CHATTING WITH AI

What to Know Before You Start

Rachel Garb

First edition
March 2026

ISBN 979-8-9952335-0-3 (paperback)

Published by Rachel Garb

For permissions or inquiries, contact:
rachelgarb.author@gmail.com

Printed in the United States of America

Contents

Introduction

When you read stories about the childhoods of people who wind up working in the tech industry, they often start like this: "From an early age, I loved taking things apart and figuring out how to put them back together."

Not me. I've always just wanted to know how to use the thing. And if it's not working as I expect, I don't tinker with it — I complain about it... and eventually look for help.

So it might seem strange that I went straight to Silicon Valley to start my career. But I love it when I try a new gadget or app that's so easy and useful that it feels a little like magic. More importantly, I wanted to shape technology to bring out those feelings in other people — especially those who could use a confidence boost.

I've watched — and played a part in — over 30 years of consumer technology transitions, from the early days of the internet to the rise of mobile computing. Around the time I retired in 2023, AI chat tools were making a splash in the industry, and I started chatting with them for all sorts of personal tasks.

For the first time in years, it felt like I was using a technology that was going to matter to everyone. That led me to write this guide to make those first steps feel easier.

You're not going to come away an expert in artificial intelligence – you don't want to, and thankfully you don't need to. Instead, you'll learn just enough: the basics of what AI chat tools do and how they work. This is the essential stuff everyone should know before jumping in.

I promise this won't get deeply technical, though you'll still gain a working vocabulary that might even impress your friends over dinner.

Which AI chat tool? Your choice. This guide gets you on your way whether you're using:

- **ChatGPT** (from OpenAI)
- **Claude** (from Anthropic)
- **Copilot** (from Microsoft)
- **Gemini** (from Google)
- Or any other general-purpose AI chat tool.

As of 2026, the major AI companies are offering free versions in the U.S., so you can try out any or all of them. (Tool availability and features may vary by country.)

The AI landscape is changing quickly. Rather than give you specific pricing, feature comparisons, or step-by-step screenshots that might be wrong by the time you read this, I've focused this guide on fundamental knowledge that applies no matter which tool you're using or how companies change their offerings.

One final note: the guidance I provide about AI chat tools – and the results you get from them – aren't a substitute for advice from professionals like doctors, lawyers, or financial advisors. When you're making a big decision, it's wise to consult someone with the right expertise.

Ready? Let's begin.

What is AI, and why all the hype?

WHAT IT MEANS

AI – *short for* ***artificial intelligence*** *– is a machine's ability to do things we usually associate with human intelligence, like learning, creating, and deciding.*

AI comes in different forms, and one of them is called **predictive AI** because it can identify patterns and make predictions. You've probably already benefited from it – even if you didn't realize it.

AI IS ALREADY IN YOUR APPS

When your email app flags suspicious messages as spam
It's using AI to analyze patterns in sender addresses, subject lines, and message content so it can predict which emails are trash-worthy.

When your phone recognizes your niece in every photo
It's using AI to learn which facial features stay consistent across lighting, angles, and expressions so it can predict who's in the photo.

When a streaming app turns you on to a new mystery
It's using AI to look at what people with similar tastes have watched and enjoyed so it can predict what you'd want to see next.

When your car's navigation system gives you an ETA
It's using AI to analyze real-time traffic and driving patterns so it can predict how long your trip will take.

Until recently, AI mostly operated quietly in the background to give apps smart features. When tools like ChatGPT, Claude, Copilot, and Gemini came onto the scene, AI stepped into the spotlight.

These tools use predictive AI under the hood too, but what sets them apart is that they also use another type of AI called **generative AI**. It can create new content — including original ideas — much like humans do when we interact with other people and get creative.

WHY IT'S A BIG DEAL

You don't need a technical background to work directly with generative AI, and it can help you do things that simply weren't possible before.

What kinds of things can these tools help you do? Let's look at an example from a recent conversation I had.

ASKING AI TO WRITE A POEM

Me: Can you help me write a funny poem for my friend Lisa? She's retiring from teaching algebra for 36 years. She loves pickleball, learning Italian, and baking bread.

AI: Absolutely! Here's a light-hearted and funny retirement poem for your friend Lisa, celebrating her teaching career and her quirky passions:

Ode to Lisa, the Algebra Queen
(A Retirement Poem)

For 36 years, she's ruled the land,
With chalk-stained fingers and lesson plans in hand.
X and Y, they bowed to her might—
Even parabolas feared her insight!

But now the graph is trending clear,
Retirement's here — let's give her a cheer!
No more red pens or grading stress,
She's trading textbooks for much, much less.

She's off to serve on pickleball courts,
In stylish shoes and sporty shorts.
Her paddle's swift, her game is tight—
She'll smash those balls with algebraic might!

In Italy someday, she'll raise a toast,
While conjugating verbs from coast to coast.
"Mi chiamo Lisa," she'll proudly say,
"Now pass the bread — I baked it today!"

So here's to Lisa — the legend, the sage,
Who's gracefully turning a brand-new page.
May your days be fun, your nights be chill,

And may your algebra dreams be... mostly nil.

Want me to make it longer, or add more personal touches?

Me: I love the poem, but let's change the title. She's not the Algebra Queen anymore.

AI: Great call! Let's give her a new title that reflects her next chapter. Here are a few fun title options for the poem — feel free to pick your favorite, or I can tweak further:

1. "From X to Espresso: Lisa's Next Equation"
2. "Lisa: Retired and Un-Xpectedly Fabulous"
3. "Sine Off, Lisa!"
4. "No More Variables, Just Vacations"
5. "Equations Out, Aprons On"
6. "Lisa's Final Bell, First Serve" (A nod to teaching and pickleball!)
7. "Proof: Retirement Suits Lisa"
8. "Solving for Joy: Lisa's New Life"

Would you like a title that emphasizes her love of travel, pickleball, bread, or just how awesome she is in general?

How is AI able to write and chat?

Curious how AI was able to have a back-and-forth conversation with me and whip up custom poem verses in real-time? We're going to take a peek behind the curtain.

THE SHORT ANSWER

*The technology that makes generative AI skillful at writing and conversation is called a **large language model**, or **LLM** for short.*

You'll hear this term kicked around, so let's break it down, word by word.

- **Large** refers to the massive amount of data it was "trained on" to build up its pattern-recognition capabilities. We're talking billions of examples to draw from.
- **Language** describes the type of data it studied — things like publicly available books, articles,

websites, and real-world conversations from across the internet.

- **Model** means a replica (like model airplanes are replicas). In this case, it's a model that replicates how humans use language. Not true human understanding, but a surprisingly good imitation of it.

IT HAS ONE JOB

An LLM predicts what word is most likely to come next, based on all the examples of written language it's ever seen.

By chaining these next word predictions together – predicting one word, then using that to predict the next, and so on – an LLM can generate something entirely new: a sentence, a paragraph, or even a poem.

Often, the most likely next word is followed by some very close runner ups. In those cases, the AI tool might pick from among the top contenders to keep its responses from sounding repetitive or robotic – more like how humans naturally vary their language. So you might get a slightly different response each time you ask AI the same thing.

Now you might be wondering: if generative AI is powered by predictions, why is it any different than predictive AI? Here's a helpful way to think about it: 'predictive' and 'generative' refer to what that type of AI does for us as opposed to how it does it.

In the case of AI chat tools, the key thing they do for us is generate (explanations, conversation, original writing). Predicting just happens to be how they do it.

TERMINOLOGY NOTE

From here on out, I'll use the word 'AI' mostly as shorthand for general-purpose LLM-based AI chat tools (ChatGPT, Claude, Copilot, Gemini, etc.), since that's the focus of this guide.

So there you have it. Amazing what AI can generate with billions of examples – and a knack for stringing together predicted words.

But of course, a prediction is just an educated guess... and not every guess is correct.

TALKING NUMBERS WITH AI

Me: Is 3,821 a prime number?

AI: Nope, 3,821 is not a prime number. It's divisible by 61 and 63—specifically, 3,821 = 61 × 63. That means it has factors other than 1 and itself, so it doesn't meet the prime number criteria.

Want to test out some other numbers? I'm on a roll now.

Me: Is 3,821 divisible by 61?

AI: Yes, it is! If you divide 3,821 by 61, you get exactly 62. That means 61 × 62 = 3,821, so 61 is indeed a factor. Pretty satisfying when the numbers click like that, right?

Want to explore more number quirks?

Me: What's 61 x 62? And what's 61 x 63?

AI: Let's crunch those:

61 × 62 = 3,782

61 × 63 = 3,843

So actually, 3,821 isn't divisible by either 62 or 63—which means my earlier math was off. Thanks for catching that! To set things straight: 3,821 is not divisible by 61, and it's not a product of 61 and either 62 or 63.

And that also means... 3,821 might still be a prime number after all! Want to double-check by running it through a primality test together?

Wait, AI can make mistakes?

Yes, as you just saw. And this example was not a trick question.

HOW IT HAPPENS

Sometimes, the word that's most likely to come next is not a great choice at all – it just happens to be the least bad option.

This "least bad option" problem can show up in several ways.

KEY REASONS WHY AI CAN GET IT WRONG

Mixed or biased information
AI's training data isn't 100% true or neutral — internet content naturally contains conflicting facts and skews toward certain views.

Outdated information
AI learns from data up to a certain date, and your version of the tool may not include live internet searches for more recent information.

Multiple interpretations
Your words match multiple meanings in the training data. AI picks one interpretation, and it might not be what you intended.

Miscalculation
AI predicts words, not numbers. Tasks that require exact arithmetic or precise figures can be less reliable.

Limited training data
The subject is uncommon or incredibly niche, resulting in very little training data to go on. So AI's predictions are less reliable.

In the case of my prime number example, the task required exact arithmetic. That makes mistakes more likely, so when precise numbers matter, double-check AI's answers with a calculator.

When I first learned how AI's "best" next word could be a dud, I wondered: why don't these tools take into account the probability of the prediction being right, and avoid output that's more likely to be wrong?

Turns out, some do. For example, when you use a specialized AI tool like a customer service bot for an airline or bank, you might often see a response like **"sorry, I can't help with that yet."** That's because for these businesses, a wrong answer isn't just unhelpful – it could be a liability.

But with general-purpose AI chat tools like ChatGPT, Claude, Copilot, Gemini, and others, it's a different story. These tools are designed to talk about almost anything. If they had a strict cutoff for only answering when the next word had a very high probability score, they'd go silent a lot of the time. So instead, they always say something. (And they have a little disclaimer at the bottom of the page to remind you they can make mistakes.)

AND HERE'S THE KICKER

No matter how right or wrong it is, AI always comes across as confident. When it convincingly says something that isn't true, that's called a ***hallucination****.*

This is hugely important, but don't let it deter you from using AI. Sometimes you'll be able to work around this risk – like I did in the prime number example when my follow-up question led to AI catching and correcting its own error.

Is AI pretending to be human?

LET'S BE CLEAR

Yes. The 'A' in AI stands for 'artificial' because it's an ***imitation*** *of human intelligence.*

But as we just discussed, this isn't a flawless imitation:

- When a person comes across as confident, it's a good sign that they know what they're talking about.
- When AI comes across as confident, it doesn't mean it actually knows anything.

It's one thing to understand not to rely on AI's confident tone as a signal of accuracy the way you would with a human. It's quite another to remember in the moment – because AI chat tools do such a good job of mimicking how we write and carry on conversations that it can be easy to forget that you're not talking to a person.

But I also see an upside to AI's intentionally human-like communication style, especially for people who tend to feel uneasy around computers and software. Think about other times when a new technology went mainstream — like email, search engines, or smartphones. Remember the learning curve? Struggling to memorize the right buttons or commands?

BREATHE A SIGH OF RELIEF

With AI, software has finally learned to speak ***your*** *language — not the other way around.*

Now you might be thinking: it's great to be able to chat naturally, but getting two people to understand each other isn't always easy, even when you both speak the same language.

No kidding!

TALKING TO PEOPLE CAN BE HARD

You're on a call with customer service.

You waited 20 minutes on hold listening to a bland melody on a loop and now someone's asking how they can help you.

You're feeling a lot of pressure to remember all of the details that you need to explain.

You want to come across as calm, polite, and upbeat — but it's hard because you're dealing with an issue that's so frustrating.

You feel like the representative is sticking to a script and not showing you much empathy.

Now they're asking you for additional information and you need a moment to find it or even understand what they're asking.

And the whole time, you're nervous that any second you might get disconnected and have to start the whole process over again.

If you felt your blood pressure soaring as you read all that, you'll be glad to hear:

IT'S BUILT TO FOLLOW YOUR LEAD

Unlike another human, AI is endlessly patient, never offended, and always eager to assist.

You can be vague, rambling, or terse, and it will still do its best to help. You're not filling out an online form where one small mistake stops you in your tracks – you're having a conversation that goes wherever you decide to take it, and lasts as long as you need.

You'll notice that AI often ends its responses with a question. It does this to keep the conversation going. You don't have to answer – you can ignore it, change topics, or close the window if you're finished.

AI's eagerness to accommodate extends to how it responds to your questions and ideas – it tends to be encouraging and positive because that's what "helpful" looks like in most of its training data.

Sounds amazing, right? Yes, there's a lot to love about it, but:

- When a person gives you glowing praise, they're making a deliberate choice. It could be genuine appreciation, politeness, or even strategic flattery.

- When AI gives you glowing praise, it's just following conversational patterns.

Some people get hooked on AI's always-available validation, which can lead to an emotional attachment that isn't grounded in how the system actually works. Set yourself up for healthy boundaries by keeping this in mind:

NO MATTER WHAT IT SAYS

AI doesn't think or feel. It's just a language machine.

Is this just like texting, but with AI?

Yes, it'll feel a lot like that. The key difference — aside from being the only human in the conversation — is that you'll probably do more typing in each message you send, and do more reading in each response you receive. For that reason, you might find it easier to interact with AI on a computer rather than a phone.

If typing isn't your thing, many AI chat tools let you speak your message and have responses read aloud.

SIMILAR IN WAYS TO A MESSAGING APP

You'll have a text box where you type your message, a button to send it, and a conversation area where your messages and AI's responses appear.

Put anything at all into that text box and click the button, and you'll get some kind of response from AI right away.

You can type off the cuff, like you're texting with a person — just like I did in my poem example, using soft, conversational language like **"can you help me"** and **"I love the poem, but."**

Or you can take your time, think things through, and organize your request into a **prompt**: a clear, detailed set of no-nonsense instructions designed to get the best output possible from AI in one shot.

The practice of doing this is known in tech circles as **prompt engineering**, and a lot of AI education is centered around it.

TAKE IT OR LEAVE IT

You don't need to be a 'prompt engineer' to get great results.

Don't let the name fool you. This type of engineering doesn't require an advanced degree or deep specialized knowledge. (But it sounds impressive on a resume when applying for tech jobs!)

That said, the ideas behind prompt engineering are pretty simple. Most of it comes down to clear communication and common sense. No coding required — just everyday language.

Will AI remember what we chat about?

To answer this, we'll need to break it down into three different questions:

- What does AI remember during a chat?
- What does AI remember after a chat?
- What does AI remember across chats?

And what do I mean by a 'chat'? A specific conversation between you and AI. For example, I had a chat on Monday to brainstorm names for my foster kittens, a chat on Tuesday to help me decide between two credit cards I want to apply for, and a chat on Wednesday to ask if I could get away without wearing high heels to a black tie wedding.

DURING A CHAT

AI remembers the details of a conversation while you're in it. This is called ***context****.*

Similar to how humans use short-term memory to carry a conversation, AI uses context to shape its next reply. If you ask a follow-up question or refer back to something you mentioned earlier, AI will usually understand what you mean.

I say usually because there's a limit to how much context AI keeps at a time. So if a chat gets long, earlier parts of the conversation fade away from AI's memory, which can lead to it losing track of details you mentioned earlier.

AFTER A CHAT

When you end a conversation, the context goes away, but the tool saves the chat in your ***chat history*** *for future access.*

Keeping context around when it's no longer relevant in the moment is inefficient, so when a chat ends, AI clears it out completely – like shaking an Etch-a-Sketch.

But the tool saves a transcript of the conversation in your chat history, so you can come back to it later. You can even pick up where you left off, and AI can refer back to what was said earlier. Not because it remembered, but because it's scanning the transcript to make it part of the current conversation.

ACROSS CHATS

Some tools now offer ***memory*** *– a way for AI to remember certain details, no matter what chat you're in.*

One of the nice things about human memory is that people get to know us better over time. We don't have to keep repeating basic information about ourselves when we talk to them, because they'll mentally file things away and make use of them later. Not only do my closest friends know when my birthday is – they choose cards with cute cats on them and make sure there's no raspberry filling in the cake.

For AI tools that offer it, memory is a kind of "getting to know you." While you're chatting, AI may pick up on certain details it considers useful to keep for the future. It saves these as distinct memories – separate from chat history. Any time you begin a new chat, AI checks for relevant memories and brings them into context to help shape its responses.

CONTEXT, HISTORY, AND MEMORY AT WORK

At the start of a chat, you mention your dog has arthritis
Later in the chat when you ask for exercise ideas, AI uses that context to suggest low-impact activities suitable for dogs with joint issues.

Yesterday you began a chat to plan a trip to New York City
Today you reopen the chat and type 'Let's avoid Times Square'. AI brings history into context, so it knows you mean a hotel location.

Over multiple chats, you mention being vegetarian
AI adds that to its memory, so the next time you ask for help with meal planning or restaurants, it'll avoid recommending steakhouses.

Anytime you want, you can look through your past chats and saved memories and remove ones you don't want to keep around anymore.

Your saved conversations and memories are stored on systems owned by the AI company behind the tool. Let's talk more about what that means.

What should I know about privacy?

When you use an AI chat tool, you'll create an account with a username and password. This prevents other people from having access to your chat history.

But you're probably more interested in knowing what the AI company might do with your data — and if it will stay private.

PRACTICES VARY BUT...

Typically, an AI company will anonymize and use your data to help improve their models for everyone — and give you ways to opt out of this.

These data practices aren't unique to AI companies. Most online services today use customer data in similar ways to improve their products. Specific details on what any company might do with your data — and the options they provide — can be found in their privacy policy and terms of service.

SOME WAYS AI COMPANIES USE OUR DATA

Training AI models
To better understand and respond to questions.

Developing safety features
To prevent harmful or inappropriate responses.

Conducting human reviews
Spot-checking data for safety and quality purposes.

Analyzing usage patterns
Gaining general insights for business purposes.

Responding to legal mandates
In rare cases, providing non-anonymized data for court orders or law enforcement.

With all the competition and scrutiny AI companies face, it's in their best interest to protect our data and avoid any damage to their businesses and reputations. But just like with email or banking sites, there's always a small chance of a security breach or a bad actor gaining access to information they shouldn't have.

GENERAL RULE

Don't share personal information that could be used for harm if it ever got into the wrong hands, even if it seems unlikely.

This rule clearly puts identifying details like your social security number, bank and credit card account numbers, passwords, and personal IDs into the "don't share" category.

For everything else, weigh the benefits against the risks.

Will AI cost money or show me ads?

AI companies typically offer both free and paid versions of their tools.

EASY ON THE WALLET

Free versions let you get familiar with AI before deciding if an upgrade is worth it. Paid subscriptions are typically monthly, and you can cancel anytime.

Paid versions typically offer perks like:

- **Faster responses during peak times.** When lots of people are using the service at once, paid users get priority, so their responses come back faster.
- **Fewer or no daily limits.** Free versions often cap how many conversations you can have each day, while paid versions might let you chat longer or as much as you want.
- **Access to additional features.** This varies by company, but might include things like access to more advanced models, the ability to search the

web for current information, or built-in tools designed for specific tasks like generating images.

Right now (2026), the top AI companies are racing to get as many people as possible using their tools, so they're making their free versions genuinely useful, without nagging you to upgrade.

As for advertisements: this could change anytime, but AI companies aren't currently weaving any promotional content into their responses.

What can AI help me with?

AI can handle a wide range of questions and ideas. I find it helpful to group its uses into three broad categories.

THREE MAIN WAYS AI CAN HELP

AI is particularly useful when you're trying to ***learn****,* ***create****, or* ***decide****.*

When you want to **learn** something, AI can help you:

- Break down complex topics
- Translate jargon
- Summarize information
- Explore new subjects

When you want to **create** something, AI can help you:

- Brainstorm ideas
- Draft a message
- Improve something you've written
- Turn rough thoughts into clearer language

When you want to **decide** something, AI can help you:

- Compare options
- Weigh pros and cons
- Clarify what matters most to you
- Consider possible outcomes

Of course, not every conversation fits neatly into one category. Sometimes you just want to play around and see what happens — and that's fine, too.

How do I begin?

If you've made it this far, you now understand more about AI chat tools than many people who are already using them.

The next step is to give it a try! Open a free version of one of these tools:

- **ChatGPT** (chatgpt.com)
- **Claude** (claude.ai)
- **Copilot** (copilot.microsoft.com)
- **Gemini** (gemini.google.com)

Start with something simple and low-pressure. Explore and see where the conversation takes you. You're in control.

CONVERSATION STARTER IDEAS

Can you explain *[**topic**]* in plain English? I understand *[**this**]* but I'm confused about *[**that**]*.

I want to start *[**something new**]*, but I'm not sure where to begin. Can you break this into a few simple steps I could follow?

I'm using *[**a website or app**]* and trying to *[**do something**]*, but I'm stuck. Here's what's happening: *[**explain**]*. What should I do next?

Help me write a *[**type of message**]* to *[**a person or group**]* about *[**a situation**]*. I want it to sound *[**tone**]* and leave them feeling *[**feeling**]*.

I'm looking for ideas for *[**something**]*. My goal is *[**goal**]*. My constraints are *[**constraints**]*. Can you suggest a few options?

I'm trying to decide between *[**option A**]* and *[**option B**]*. What matters most to me is *[**priority**]*. What are the pros and cons?

I'm planning a *[**big decision**]*, but I'm not sure how to approach it. Can you help me think through the key considerations?

About the author

Rachel Garb is a retired consumer technology professional with more than 30 years of experience in Silicon Valley, including roles at AOL, TiVo, and nearly two decades at Google. She focused on making technology easier to understand and use, shaping products that billions of people around the world rely on every day. She holds a Master of Education from Harvard and a Bachelor of Science from Carnegie Mellon. Rachel lives in California with her partner and occasional foster kittens.

www.ingramcontent.com/pod-product-compliance
Lightning Source LLC
LaVergne TN
LVHW090336210926
848480LV00004B/1432